FROM THE LIBRARY OF

· · · · · · · · · · · · · · · ·

May Out West

Also by May Swenson

May Out West

poems of May Swenson

UTAH STATE UNIVERSITY PRESS
Logan, Utah

Utah State University Press
Logan, Utah   84322-7800

Typography by WolfPack

Library of Congress Cataloging-in-Publication Data
Swenson, May.
  May out west : poems of May Swenson.
    p.   cm.
  ISBN 0–87421–200–6
  I. Title.
PS3537.W4786M39 199
811'.54--dc20   95-41762
                                                                       CIP

The poems "The Seed of My Father" and "White Mood" are published here for the first time.
Several poems are collected here for the first time, but were previously published as follows: in
    American Poetry Review, "Something Goes By"; in *The New Yorker*, "Memory of the Future?
    Prophecy of the Past?" and "My Name Was Called"; in *Parnassus,* "Night Visits with the Family
    II"; in *Poetry*, "Overview"; in *The Raven Anthology*, "Nightly Vision."
Other poems were previously published as indicated.
    in *Iconographs*. Copyright © 1970 by May Swenson. "My Face the Night."
    in *New and Selected Things Taking Place*. Copyright © 1978 by May Swenson. "Night Visits
        with the Family" and "That the Soul May Wax Plump."
    in *In Other Words*. Copyright © 1987 by May Swenson. Reprinted by permission of Alfred A.
        Knopf Inc. All rights reserved. "Morning at Point Dume," "Saguaros Above Tucson,"
        "Summerfall."
    in *American Sports Poems*, compiled by R.R. Knudson and May Swenson. Copyright © 1988
        by R.R. Knudson. "Bronco Busting, Event #1."
    in *The Complete Poems to Solve*. Copyright © 1993 by The Literary Estate of May Swenson.
        Reprinted with the permission of Simon & Schuster Books for Young Readers. All rights
        reserved. "The Centaur."
    in *The Wonderful Pen of May Swenson*. Copyright © 1993 by R.R. Knudson and the Literary
        Estate of May Swenson. Reprinted with the permission of Simon & Schuster Books for
        Young Readers. All rights reserved. "The Exchange."
    in *Nature*. Copyright © 1994 by The Literary Estate of May Swenson. Reprinted by permission
        of Houghton Mifflin Co. All rights reserved. "Above Bear Lake", "Bison Crossing Near
        Mt. Rushmore", "Beast", "Camping in Madera Canyon", "Cumuli", "A Day is Laid By",
        "Digging in the Garden of Age I Uncover a Live Root", "Earth Your Dancing Place", "Feel
        Me", "Flying Home from Utah", "Goodnight", "Haymaking", "I Look at My Hand", "The
        North Rim", "A Navajo Blanket", "The Poplar's Shadow", "Speed."

Contents

May Out West

These poems were selected and arranged by R.R. Knudson, who dedicates the collection to May's faithful sisters and brothers—Grace, Ruth, Beth, Margaret, Roy, Dan, George, and Paul.

***

For generous financial support of this collection, thanks to the College of Humanities, Arts, and Social Sciences at Utah State University, of which May Swenson was a distinguished graduate.

Above Bear Lake

Sky and lake the same blue,
and blue the languid mountain between them.
Cloud fluffs make the scene flow.
Greeny white poles of aspen snake up,
graven with welts and calluses where branches
dried and broke. Other scabs are lover-made:
initials dug within linked hearts and, higher,
some jackknifed peace signs.
A breeze, and the filtered light makes shine
a million bristling quills of spruce and fir
downslope, where slashes of sky and lake
hang blue—windows of intense stain. We take
the rim trail, crushing bloom of sage,
sniffing resinous wind, our boots in the wild,
small, everycolored Rocky Mountain flowers.
Suddenly, a steep drop-off: below we see the whole,
the whale of it—deep, enormous blue—
that widens, while the sky slants back to pale
behind a watercolored mountain.
Western Tanager—we call him "Fireface"—
darts ahead, we climb to our camp
as the sun slips lower. Clipped to the top
of the tallest fir, Olive-sided Flycatcher,
over and over, fierce-whistles, "Whip!
Whip three bears! Whip, whip three bears!"

The Centaur

The summer that I was ten—
Can it be there was only one
summer that I was ten? It must

have been a long one then—
each day I'd go out to choose
a fresh horse from my stable

which was a willow grove
down by the old canal.
I'd go on my two bare feet.

But when, with my brother's jack-knife,
I had cut me a long limber horse
with a good thick knob for a head,

and peeled him slick and clean
except a few leaves for the tail,
and cinched my brother's belt

around his head for a rein,
I'd straddle and canter him fast
up the grass bank to the path,

trot along in the lovely dust
that talcumed over his hoofs,
hiding my toes, and turning

his feet to swift half-moons.
The willow knob with the strap
jouncing between my thighs

was the pommel and yet the poll
of my nickering pony's head.
My head and my neck were mine,

yet they were shaped like a horse.
My hair flopped to the side
like the mane of a horse in the wind.

My forelock swung in my eyes,
my neck arched and I snorted.
I shied and skittered and reared,

stopped and raised my knees,
pawed at the ground and quivered.
My teeth bared as we wheeled

and swished through the dust again.
I was the horse and the rider,
and the leather I slapped to his rump

spanked my own behind.
Doubled, my two hoofs beat
a gallop along the bank,

the wind twanged in my mane,
my mouth squared to the bit.
And yet I sat on my steed

quiet, negligent riding,
my toes standing the stirrups,
my thighs hugging his ribs.

At a walk we drew up to the porch.
I tethered him to a paling.
Dismounting, I smoothed my skirt

and entered the dusky hall.
My feet on the clean linoleum
left ghostly toes in the hall.

Where have you been? said my mother.
Been riding, I said from the sink,
and filled me a glass of water.

What's that in your pocket? she said.
Just my knife. It weighted my pocket
and stretched my dress awry.

Go tie back your hair, said my mother,
and *Why is your mouth all green?*
*Rob Roy, he pulled some clover
as we crossed the field,* I told her.

Memory of the Future?
Prophecy of the Past?

I

A structure that haunts memory. Its bulk,
outline, height and darkness, its shining
edges. The thick pillars hatted black,
their heads of puffed charcoal or caps
of soot on quenched matches magnified or
Charlie Chaplin's bowler of felt that's
felt by the fingertips of the eyes, that
exact soft roughness. An edifice all of
hollow wood. Between its squat black
pillars slim flute-shaped pipes burnished gold.
From their chiselled slits are blown the every-
colored streamers, the lacy delicate swells
of sound. Then, overwhelming, from under-
ground roots of the pillars, thunderous
quakes and guttural groans reverberate.
In a semicircular embrace, tier on tier
are skulls and torsos, an enormous chorus
that is a terraced garden of pastel
females, sombre males, whose throats,
uniting, strum and shudder, an expanding
avalanche of sound. Broad-striped
skywide harmonies concatenate, dissonant
and sweet, a peppered honey. Phalanxes
of rainbows, transparent tender colors
bloom on the ear's horizon. Interpene-
trating tones inundate the sprawling
strands of the nerves, sluggish

blood jumps to injected spurts of lightning,
the flood suddenly buttressed by brutal
final tomb-deep chords of climax. During
the stun of silence a whole minute,
interminable as a hundred years, before
reversal and rollback of echoes finally
complete themselves and die.

II

It is before I can walk. I sit on the floor,
a vast vaguely patterned rug stretching to
the borders of the room. I hold a book whose
pages are of cloth, the edges serrated as if
with pinking shears. Picture books that could
not be torn were given to babies then.
I love my soft book, each page of which shows
an animal. Turning the pages I have come
to Elephant. Gray and huge, his trunk
is raised, tip facing me, held up like
a curled cup. There are words in a row under
the Elephant. I cannot yet read. I don't
need to. I know everything by looking.
There is warmth around me. I am not alone.
The legs of my parents encase me where they sit
together on a couch behind me. I know that
Father is on my left and Mother on my right.
A steady light permeates the room, not bright,
not gloomy—a lasting-forever light,
neither night nor day. I have on a white
dress and white socks. I think I have not yet
seen color. I feel the cotton softness of
the book's cover and pages, their smoothness
but also the slight ridges of threads
between my thumbs and forefingers.

Elephant's trunk, its tip erect,
thrust forward, a nose that is also lips
that suck in, blow out, that gropes like a paw
and seems to see with nostrils, that
might be eyes looking at me. Elephant.
This is my first memory.

Beast

my Brown self
goes on four paws
supple-twining in the
lewd Gloom

arching against the
shaggy hedges
with a relishing Purr
tasting among his
spurted fur

the Ripeness
brisk and willing
of his brown body

yawning Obscurely
glittered-glancing
couching himself
in the sunny places

beating his tail
where traces
of She-odor make
a pattern for
his unbrained thought

feeling the Budding
thorns in his
feet of felt

planning to Stab them
into the wincing pelt
of a creature smaller

my Brown self
a thing gleam-jawed
goes downright
Four-pawed

Something Goes By

What are you doing?
I'm watching myself watch myself.

And what are you doing?
Pushing a stick, with a wooden wheel at the end.
I have on a white dress.
First I push the wheel, then I pull the wheel.
My dad made it, with the lathe and a bandsaw.

And where are you watching from?
From my seat on the train.
My back is to myself, back there. But with the back
of my head I'm watching myself:
on a strip of cement, by a square of grass,
pushing the wheel that isn't quite round,
so it wobbles and clacks.

I'm crossing a trestle over a river on the train . . .
the water's gray and level there below,
with stroke-marks on it, in arm-length arcs,
like wet cement that's just been planed.
My dad built our house, poured concrete for the basement,
sawed timber for the frame, laid the brick,
put on the roof, shingle by shingle,
lying along the ladder with nails in his mouth,
plastered the inside, laid the floorboards,
made our furniture out of wood:
of wave-grained oak our dining table . . .
my round, high stool he scooped in the center just like a saucer . . .

There's a hat on my lap that I mustn't leave on the train,
new shoes on my feet, that fuse my toes to flatiron shape.
I'm watching myself being carried away.

And where are you watching from?
From *here*. From out of a slit of almost sleep . . .
lying on my side,
hands between my knees.
I hear myself breathe.
My bed is a dais in the hollow room;
in the window frame a section of sky:
slow clouds puff by, over the city, on a track from the west—
like an endless—is it an endless?—train.
I hear an airplane being driven into heaven,
its drone the saw-sound, the sound
of the lathe—or is it the rasp of my own
breath in my ear?
When I look to the window, will it be gone—
or moved to another wall? Will it be dawn
in another room?—Or in this same
room in another year?—Already I hear
November horns on the river.

Where is here?
And what are you doing?
I'm running,
and pushing something.
I have on a white dress.
I'm sitting,
and something carries me.
There's a hat on my lap.
I'm lying naked, almost asleep . . .
Some
thing
goes
by.

Haymaking

The sagging hayricks file into the lane
The horses' chests are wading
toward home and evening
Today they gather summer to the barns
The lean-hipped men in aisles of stubble
lurching pitch whole yellow acres
the sun astride their necks all day

Now they rock in tousled cradles
Sweat-dark reins lace idle fingers
Soon to taste evening on the tongue
Evening will smooth their eyelids

By forkfulls they gather summer in
to heap in the cool barns
Snug against the rafters pile the
yellow stuff of summer
Against the crisp walls press
the sweet grasses
Bed down the loft with a shaggy mattress
and line the shady stalls where butterflies
drift through the knotholes

So when winter whistles in the bee
and frets the willow
of her last ragged leaf
when snow leans in the doorsill
at the steaming crib the cow
will munch on summer

With brown bemused stare
pools and pasture shade
juicy banks of green she'll conjure
and absently will wag an ear
at droning memory's fly

White Mood

Tonight
within my brain no bell
only the snowing
of my thoughts

Flake on flake
sharp and white
snow my thoughts
against the night

In tall silence
the snowdunes deepen
swerving
fingered by wind

Shadow-stroked and blue
my thoughts are heaped
and swerve
even as snow

One word were it spoken
would take black shape
like a footprint
in the naked snowdune

But no word is born
no bell swings
in the steeple
of my brain

Cumuli

Is it St. Peter's or St. Paul's this dome
reminds you of?
This blue enameled basin upside down
is it of London Luxembourg or Rome?

Would Blake know how to call it pure
yet grand
Would Shakespeare standing where I stand
compare these clouds to Michelangelo?

I have never traveled never seen
those treasure piles of history hewn
to the golden mean
art more ravishing than nature
fabled yield
gemmed sediment of centuries

This Western field under the summer noon
with sibilent lucerne sown
columned with poplars is my Parthenon
On immense blue
around its vaulted walls
alabaster shapes inhabit beauty's pedestals

Earth Your Dancing Place

Beneath heaven's vault
remember always walking
through halls of cloud
down aisles of sunlight
or through high hedges
of the green rain
walk in the world
highheeled with swirl of cape
hand at the swordhilt
of your pride
Keep a tall throat
Remain aghast at life

Enter each day
as upon a stage
lighted and waiting
for your step
Crave upward as flame
have keenness in the nostril
Give your eyes
to agony or rapture

Train your hands
as birds to be
brooding or nimble
Move your body
as the horses

sweeping on slender hooves
over crag and prairie
with fleeing manes
and aloofness of their limbs

Take earth for your own large room
and the floor of earth
carpeted with sunlight
and hung round with silver wind
for your dancing place

The Seed of my Father

I rode on his shoulder. He showed me the moon.
He told me its name with a kiss in my ear.
"My moon," I said. "Yours," he agreed.
And as we walked, it followed us home.

Holding my hand, he showed me a tree,
and picked a peach, and let me hold it.
I took a bite, then he took a bite.
"Ours?" I asked. "Yes, our tree."
Then with a hoe he made the water flow beside it.

When I was older he showed me the sun.
He made me a wooden wheel on a stick,
of pine wood, raw and bright as the sun.
I used to run and roll it.

A flashing circular saw was the sun,
like the one he made my wheel with.
"This little wheel belongs to me, the big one
to you?" "Yes," he agreed, "just as we
belong to the sun."

He let me plant the corn grains one by one
out of a long hollow slip-box thrust in the ground.
"I who plant seeds for my father,
I am the seed of my father."

And when the corn was tall, it swallowed me up, all,
whispering over my head. "You are the seed of your father."
And when the husks were sere, my father with a rake,
in the cold time of the year, made a bush of gold.

He struck the bush to burning for my sake.
I stood at his shoulder, a little the higher.
I was the seed of my father, my father
outlined by the fire.

He made a garden, and he planted me.
Sun and moon he named and deeded to me.
Water and fire he created, created me,
he named me into being: I am the seed of my father.

His breath he gave me, he gave me night and day.
His universe is in me fashioned from his clay.
I feed on the juice of the peach from his eternal tree.
Each poem I plant is a seedling from that tree.
I plant the seed of my father.

I Look At My Hand

I look at my hand and see
it is also his and hers;
the pads of the fingers his,

the wrists and knuckles hers.
In the mirror my pugnacious eye
and ear of an elf, his;

my tamer mouth and slant
cheekbones hers.
His impulses my senses swarm,
her hesitations they gather.
Father and Mother
who dropped me,

an acorn in the wood,
repository of your shapes
and inner streams and circles,

you who lengthen toward heaven,
forgive me
that I do not throw

the replacing green
trunk when you are ash.
When you are ash, no
features shall there be,
tangled of you,
interlacing hands and faces

through me
who hide, still hard,
    far down under your shades—

          and break my root, and prune my buds,
            that what can make no replica
       may spring from me.

That the Soul May Wax Plump

He who has reached the highest degree of emptiness will
be secure in repose.

                —a Taoist saying

My dumpy little mother on the undertaker's slab
had a mannequin's grace. From chin to foot
the sheet outlined her, thin and tall. Her face
uptilted, bloodless, smooth, had a long smile.
Her head rested on a block under her nape,
her neck was long, her hair waved, upswept. But later,
at "the viewing," sunk in the casket in pink tulle,
an expensive present that might spoil, dressed
in Eden's green apron, organdy bonnet on,
she shrank, grew short again, and yellow. Who
put the gold-rimmed glasses on her shut face, who
laid her left hand with the wedding ring on
her stomach that really didn't seem to be there
under the fake lace?

Mother's work before she died was self-purification,
a regimen of near starvation, to be worthy to go
to Our Father, Whom she confused (or, more aptly, fused)
with our father, in Heaven long since. She believed
in evacuation, an often and fierce purgation,
meant to teach the body to be hollow, that the soul
may wax plump. At the moment of her death, the wind
rushed out from all her pipes at once. Throat and rectum
sang together, a galvanic spasm, hiss of ecstasy.
Then, a flat collapse. Legs and arms flung wide,
like that female Spanish saint slung by the ankles
to a cross, her mouth stayed open in a dark O. So,
her vigorous soul whizzed free. On the undertaker's slab, she
lay youthful, cool, triumphant, with a long smile.

Feel Me

"Feel me to do right," our father said on his deathbed.
We did not quite know—in fact, not at all—what he meant.
His last whisper was spent as through a slot in a wall.
He left us a key, but how did it fit? "Feel me
to do right." Did it mean that, though he died, he would be felt
through some aperture, or by some unseen instrument
our dad just then had come to know? So, to do right always,
we need but feel his spirit? Or was it merely his apology
for dying? "Feel that I do right in not trying,
as you insist, to stay on your side. There is the wide
gateway and the splendid tower, and you implore me
to wait here, with the worms!"

Had he defined his terms, and could we discriminate
among his motives, we might have found out how to "do right"
before *we* died—supposing he felt he suddenly knew
what dying was. "You do wrong because you do not feel
as I do now," was maybe the sense. "Feel me, and emulate
my state, for I am becoming less dense—I am feeling right
for the first time." And then the vessel burst,
and we were kneeling around an emptiness.

We cannot feel our father now. His power courses through us,
yes, but *he*—the chest and cheek, the foot and palm,
the mouth of oracle—is calm. And we still seek
his meaning. "Feel me," he said, and emphasized that word.
Should we have heard it as a plea for a caress—
a constant caress, since flesh to flesh was all that we

could do right if we would bless him?
The dying must feel the pressure of that question—
lying flat, turning cold from brow to heel—the hot
cowards there above protesting their love, and saying,
"What can we do? Are you all right?" While the wall opens
and the blue night pours through. "What can we do?
We want to do what's right."

"Lie down with me, and hold me, tight. Touch me. Be
with me. Feel with me. *Feel* me to do right."

Goodnight

He and the wind
She and the house

Slow from the house
whose mellow walls
have fondled him
slow from the
yellow threshold
to the purple wind

Harsh as a dog's tongue
the licking wind
upon her throat
Rough it wraps
and fondles her
as slow into the night
he walks

She and the house now only
He and the wind

Night Visits with the Family

Sharon's Dream

We were rounding up cattle, riding trees instead of horses.
The way I turned the herd was to let my tree limb grow.
Circling out around an obstinate heifer,
my horse stretched and whipped back, but too slow.

Paul's Dream

Twelve white shirts and I had to iron them.
Some swirled away. They were bundles of cloud.
Hailstones fell and landed as buttons.
I should have picked them up before they melted to mud.

Roy's Dream

Down in the cellar a library of fruit:
berries, pears and apricots published long ago.
Two lids of wax covered my eyelids. A tart title
I couldn't read was pasted on my brow.

Dan's Dream

In the playhouse Dad made when I was six
I put my captive hawk. The chimney had a lid
that locked. The wallpaper of roses was faded and fouled.
I couldn't wake, and dirty feathers filled my little bed.

Grace's Dream

Hindleg in the surf, my grand piano, groaning,
crawled ashore. I saw that most of the black keys

had been extracted, their roots were bleeding. It tried
to embrace me while falling forward on three knees.

Margaret's Dream
There was an earthquake and Jordan's boot got caught
in a crack in the street. His bike had fallen through
and went on peddling underneath, came up the basement
stairs to warn me what had happened. That's how I knew.

Betty's Dream
Aunt Etta was wearing a wig, of wilver. Its perfection
made you see how slack her chins were. Under the hair
in front was a new eye, hazel and laughing. It winked.
"You, too, will be 72," she said. It gave me a scare.

George's Dream
Old Glory rippling on a staff. No, it was a Maypole,
and the ribbons turned to rainbows. I saw a cat
climbing the iridescent bow. Then I was sliding down
a bannister. My uniform split in the crotch, I was so fat.

Corwin's Dream
With my new camera I was taking a picture of my old
camera. The new one was guaranteed: it was the kind
that issues instant color prints. What came out
was an X-Ray of the tunnel in the roller of a window blind.

Ruth's Dream
Standing under the shower I was surprised
to see I wasn't naked. The streams had dressed
me in a gown of seed pearls, and gloves that my nails
poked through like needles. They pricked if I touched my breast.

Steve's Dream

Two tiny harmonicas. I kept them in my mouth,
and sucked them. That made twin secret tunes.
Mother said, "What is it you are always humming?"
I told her they were only the stones of prunes.

Diane's Dream

Grandmother wasn't dead. Only her ring finger.
Before we buried it, we must remove the ruby.
And the finger was jack-knifed. I offered to unclench it,
but couldn't do it. I was too much of a booby.

May's Dream

Cowpuncher on a tree-horse wears
a cloud-shirt with hailstone buttons.
He rides and, through wax eyelids, reads
a library of fruit. He passes a hawk
locked in a playhouse, a grand piano
with three broken knees. Nothing he can do
about any of these. When old, an Auntie
in a wilver wig, he goes. He's almost too fat
to slide down the rainbow's banister that
ends in a gray X-Ray of a tunnel in the blind.
There he wears a water dress, tastes secret tunes.
Until I wake he cannot die. Until I wake,
the ruby lives on the dead finger.

Summerfall

After "the glorious Fourth," summer tumbles down.
An old hotel in Salt Lake City, Newhouse its name—
methodically installed with plugs of dynamite

for time-released explosion—burst!
Stupendously slow, the upper stories first. So
the whole west side of summer shears away.

Leafy cornices and balconies shatter, whirl down,
reduce to particles. The smash accelerates
as autumn's avalanches slide in planned relay,

until blanked out behind gray towers of fog.
All will be flattened. Graciousness, out of date,
must go, in instantaneous shock.

But Mind projects it slow,
stretching movement out, each flung chunk floating
awhile, weightless, and with no noise.

Mind reluctantly unbuilds summer.
The four-square, shade-roofed mansions
of an early, honest, work-proud era fall

to the dust of demolition. Prompt to come, ye Saints,
your condominiums, high-rise business, boosted
economy, new cash flow.

After "the rockets' red glare," here on the eastern shore
a sick acrylic sunset loiters in murky haze.
The sequence of such evenings will be speeding up.

Morning At Point Dume

Blond stones all round-sided,
that the tide has tumbled on sand's table,
like large warm loaves strewn in the sun.

Wet pathways drain among them, sandgrains
diamond in morning light.
A high-hipped dog trots toward the sea,

followed by a girl, naked, young,
breasts jouncing, and long fair hair.
Girl and dog in the hissing surf

roister, dive and swim together,
bodies flashing dolphin-smooth,
the hair in her delta crisp dark gold.

The Pacific is cold. Rushed ashore on a wave,
her body blushes with stings of spume.
Running upslope, the circling dog

leaps to her hand, scatters spray
from his thick blond malamute fur.
Together they twine the stone loaves' maze.

Girl lets her glistening belly down
on a yellow towel on hard hot sand,
dog panting, *couchant* by her side.

Five surfers in skintight black
rubber suits, their plexiglass
boards on shoulders, stride the shore,

their eyes searching the lustrous water
for the hills of combers that build far out,
to mount and ride the curling snowtops.

The sunburned boys in phalanx pass,
squinting ahead, scuffing sand.
Without a glance at the yellow towel

they advance to the sea.
Enormous breakers thunder in.
Falling, they shake the ground.

The Poplar's Shadow

When I was little, when
the poplar was in leaf,
its shadow made a sheaf,
the quill of a great pen
dark upon the lawn
where I used to play.

Grown, and long away
into the city gone,
I see the pigeons print
a loop in air and, all
their wings reversing, fall
with silver undertint
like poplar leaves, their seams
in the wind blown.

Time's other side, shown
as a flipped coin, gleams
on city ground
when I see a pigeon's feather:
little and large together,
the poplar's shadow is found.

Staring at here,
and superposing then,

I wait for when.
What shapes will appear?
Will great birds swing
over me like gongs?
The poplar plume belongs
to what enormous wing?

Bison Crossing Near Mt. Rushmore

There is our herd of cars stopped,
staring respectfully at the line of bison crossing.
One big-fronted bull nudges his cow into a run.
She and her calf are first to cross.
In swift dignity the dark-coated caravan sweeps through
the gap our cars leave in the two-way stall
on the road to the Presidents.
The polygamous bulls guarding their families from the rear,
the honey-brown calves trotting head-to-hip
by their mothers—who are lean and muscled as bulls,
with chin tassels and curved horns—
all leap the road like a river, and run.
The strong and somber remnant of western freedom
disappears into the rough grass of the draw,
around the point of the mountain.
The bison, orderly, disciplined by the prophet-faced,
heavy-headed fathers, threading the pass
of our awestruck stationwagons, Airstreams and trailers,
if in dread of us give no sign,
go where their leaders twine them, over the prairie.
And we keep to our line,
staring, stirring, revving idling motors, moving
each behind the other, herdlike, where the highway leads.

Speed

Winnipeg to Medicine Hat, Manitoba, Canada

In 200 miles
a tender painting
on the wind-

shield, not yet done,
in greeny yellows,
crystalline pinks,

a few smeared
browns. Fuselages
split on impact,

stuck, their juices
instantly dried. Spat-
tered flat out-

lines, superfine
strokes, tokens of
themselves flying,

frail engines
died in various
designs: mainly arrow-

shapes, wings gone,
bellies smitten
open, glaze and tincture

the wipers can't
erase. In 400 miles
a palette, thick

impasto; in 600
a palimpsest the sun
bakes through. Stained

glass, not yet done
smiting the wind-
borne, speeds on.

Overview

From above I thought
I'll understand it better
but a tender streaky skin
like the belly of a beast
rolled over to be stroked,
was cover.
Farther out
high white tufts
chimney-shaped and snarled by the wind
grew. And after that
on a level lower but still
obscuring
lay a grayer pelt,
bumpy, a melting
relief map.
(That wasn't it—was part
of its floating
skin.) Over the Great
Lakes now it is stretched
flat in the light,
all that wool sheared away.
And here's a crazy quilt of many seams,
some holes torn in the middle
frankly black and blue,
the naked water showing through,
disrupting rigid edges of the squares and pieces.

As if a great machine,
and taking centuries,
had sewn this comforter. And still
the needles work and sleep
and propagate to rework,
spreading the fabric finally to sleep
within it. So it, too, is a skin,
jigsawed and seamed,
more puzzling than the hairy
veil now clothing it again.
I do not understand it
any better, needle though I
am, privileged to stitch
above it, here, for a moment
in the clear, between it
and the sun.

A Navajo Blanket

Eye-dazzlers the Indians weave. Three colors
are paths that pull you in, and pin you
to the maze. Brightness makes your eyes jump,
surveying the geometric field. Alight, and enter
any of the gates—of Blue, of Red, of Black.
Be calmed and hooded, a hawk brought down,
glad to fasten to the forearm of a Chief.

You can sleep at the center,
attended by Sun that never fades, by Moon
that cools. Then, slipping free of zigzag and
hypnotic diamond, find your way out
by the spirit trail, a faint Green thread that
secretly crosses the border, where your mind
is rinsed and returned to you like a white cup.

The North Rim

Great dark bodies, the mountains.
Between them wriggling the canyon road,
little car, bug-eyed, beaming, goes
past ticking and snicking of August insects,
smell of sage and cedar, to a summit of stars.
Sky glints like fluorescent rock.
Cloth igloo erected, we huff up our bed,
listen to the quaking of leaf-hearts
that, myriad, shadow our sleep.

At dawn, the bodies discovered rugged, oblate,
Indian-warpaint-red, a rooster crows.
Barefoot in brickdust, we strike our tent.
Car crawls the knee of the Great White Throne.
Chiseled by giant tomahawks, the slabs.
In half-finished doorways broad gods stand.
Wind-whipped from the niches, white-throated swifts
razor the void.
We rise to ponderosa, to deer park, to moraine,
mountain bluebirds stippling the meadows,
and coast to the Grand Rim:

Angular eels of light
scribble among the buttes and crinoline
escarpments. Thunder's organ tumbles
into the stairwell of the gorge.
When rain and mist divide their veil,
westering sun, a palette knife, shoves into the cut

colors thick and bright, enclabbering
every serrate slant and vertical;
hard edged, they jut forward,
behind, beside them purple groins and pits
in shadow. Shadow within shadow beneath a shawl
of shadow darkens, and we dare not blink
till light tweaks out.

Morning at Cape Royal. A Merry-Go-Round
out there in the red cirque, Brahma's Temple.
Many Pavilions made a Great

                        Pavilion.
                 Where mountain
                    peaks eroded to flat
                      ranges, flat ranges broke
                        and parted, became pediments,
                          and pointed pediments, pinnacles, were
                    honed to skinny minarets,
or else, inverted cones, big-headed totems—
Look: On the slope a stone Boot two miles high,
the hip-end slouched in folds, some seven-leaguer
left six million years.
A lizard where I sit, with petrific eye,
is Dinosaur's little cousin
watching me from Juniper's bony root.

Two coils of the river seen from here,
muddy infinite oozing heavy paint.
Each object has its shadow. Or, if not,
must vanish. Now while the sun leans,
tabernacles form. Allow dark openings,
violet-cool arcades. Establish bases,

though colosseums, carved by the shift
of a cloud, descend pendant,
and Great sinks into shadow.
We must go. It rains. The car trickles east
over the frogback of the Kaibab Forest.
I must imagine morning, from Angel's Window
how to dive, firebrushed by the sun.

Camping in Madera Canyon

We put up our tent while the dark closed in
and thickened, the road a black trough
winding the mountain down. Leaving the lantern
ready to light on the stone table,
we took our walk. The sky was a bloom
of sharp-petaled stars.

Walls of the woods, opaque and still,
gave no light or breath or echo, until,
faint and far, a string of small toots—
nine descending notes—the whiskered owl's
signal. A tense pause . . . then, his mate's
identical reply.

At the canyon's foot, we turned,
climbed back to camp, between tall walls
of silent dark. Snugged deep into our sacks,
so only noses felt the mountain chill,
we heard the owls once more. Farther from us,
but closer to each other. The pause, that linked
his motion with her seconding, grew longer
as we drowsed. Then, expectation frayed,
we forgot to listen, slept.

In a tent, first light tickles the skin
like a straw. Still freezing cold out there,
but we in our pouches sense the immense
volcano, sun, about to pour
gold lava over the mountain, upon us.

Wriggling out, we sleepily unhinge,
make scalding coffee, shivering, stand and sip;
tin rims burn our lips.

Daybirds wake, the woods are filling
with their rehearsal flutes and pluckings,
buzzes, scales and trills. Binoculars
dangling from our necks, we walk
down the morning road. Rooms of the woods
stand open. Glittering trunks
rise to a limitless loft of blue. New snow,
a delicate rebozo, drapes the peak that,
last night, stooped in heavy shadow.

Night hid this day. What sunrise may it be
the dark to? What wider light ripens to dawn
behind familiar light? As by encircling arms
our backs are warmed by the blessing sun,
all is revealed and brought to feature.
All but the owls. The Apaches believe
them ghosts of ancestors, who build their nests
of light with straws pulled from the sun.

The whiskered owls are here, close by,
in the tops of the pines, invisible and radiant,
as we, blind and numb, awaken—our just-born
eyes and ears, our feet that walk—
as brightness bathes the road.

Bronco Busting, Event #1

The stall so tight he can't raise heels or knees
when the cowboy, coccyx to bareback, touches down

tender as a deerfly, forks him, gripping the rope-
handle over the withers, testing the cinch,

as if hired to lift a cumbersome piece of brown
luggage, while assistants perched on the rails arrange

the kicker, a foam-rubber band around the narrowest,
most ticklish part of the loins, leaning full weight

on neck and rump to keep him throttled, this horse,
"Firecracker," jacked out of the box through the sprung

gate, in the same second raked both sides of the belly
by ratchets on booted heels, bursts into five-way

motion: bucks, pitches, swivels, humps, and twists,
an all-over-body-sneeze that must repeat

until the flapping bony lump attached to his spine is gone.
A horn squawks. Up from the dust gets a buster named Tucson.

Saguaros Above Tucson

Saguaros, fuzzy and huggable, greet us, seeming to stream
down the Rincon foothills as the car climbs. Their plump
arms branch, bend upward, enthused. Each prickly person,
droll, gregarious, we would embrace, but, up close, rigid
as cast plaster, spikey, bristling—how dare we touch?
Among the palo verde, teddybear cholla, ocotillo,
bristlebush and organpipe, we meet the desert tribe,
our friends from last year, standing in place, saluting

with their many arms. Granddaddies have most, are tallest
and toughest. Great girths they display, with numerous
bulging offspring graft-on-graft attached.
Adolescents, green and comical, big cucumbers, boast only
beginning bulbs of arms. A few peculiars, single, slim,
the air private around them, stand lonely, limbless—
perhaps forever young?—Low on the ground, babies,
fat little barrels, have only heads as yet, and sprout

scarce blond quills. We'd like to stop the car, get out
and climb the flinty gullies, walk to meet these giant
innocents, our friends, say Howdy, hug, take all their
stuckout hands. But, ouch! We do not know their ritual
handshake, or how to make retract their dangerous nails.
In spring, their heads wear crowns of bloom, dainty and
festive. Flowers come out of their ears, out of fingers
and elbows come rainfresh colors, buds like blushing fruits.

Finches fix themselves in rings around the thorny brows,
whistling from rosy throats. Why are the little birds
not pierced? How do they perch so carelessly on
peaks of prickly needle-twigs?
When from freezing, lightning, windthrow or old age,
in a hundred and fifty years or more, the giants die,
they still stand. Shriveled, blackened, dried and peeling
scabby corpses, tall untouchables, they haunt the hills.

And elf owls roost in the breasts of the dead saguaros.
One moonless night last year we discovered them with
a flashlight. In a chardark hole at vestpocket height
in the ghost of an old saguaro we found round yellow eyes
crossed and weird: a tiny pale-streaked owl hunched
in a pulpy torso whose broken twists of arms, long fallen,
lay around it on the ground.
We looked for more. Still, as if stuffed, the owls stared,

framed in the cameos of our hypnotic beams aimed
at the hollow chests of the dead saguaros.
On sunny mornings this year, Rivoli's hummingbirds
will hover and snick, ignite and gyrate in their courting
dives above the tall, tough, corduroy bodies and
blooming heads of sturdy young saguaros. Again astonished,
we'll ask each other: On such stiletto-pointed pates
how is it that the elf owl mates?

Digging in the Garden of Age
I Uncover a Live Root
(For E.W.)

The smell of wet geraniums. On furry
leaves, transparent drops rounded
as cats' eyes seen sideways.
Smell of the dark earth, and damp
brick of the pots you held, tamped empty.
Flash of the new trowel. Your eyes
green in greenhouse light. Smell of
your cotton smock, of your neck
in the freckled shade of your hair.
A gleam of sweat in your lip's scoop.
Pungent geranium leaves, their wet
smell when our widening pupils met.

My Face the Night

My eyes seeing nothing
but night in my head
sent two tears south

toward inlets of my mouth.
North in the height
there swam forth two stars

as if from far pupils,
My tongue licked up two
salt drops of light.

Nightly Vision

Green river that enwraps my home
I see you twining still in dream
There is perpetual afternoon
and summer brooding by that stream

I see the clouds that pause and sit
ever above the blue-cloaked field
No wind lurks in the hissing wheat
nor night nor change the visions yield

The house and there within a room
they move (but softly as through glass
have being for the eye alone)
They move as ghosts the color of flesh

A dream of diligence confines
my footsteps to the shadowy stair
and to the green evasive lanes
that bind a house and one room there

On the mind's chaos a mirage
of windless valleys and of home
waits for the sleeper like a stage
to which he must nightly come

Night Visits With the Family II

Virginia's Dream

When I unlocked the file drawer, second from the top,
    I found an old diary from 1999.
In it was a list of Things To Do Today: Learn to hang-glide.
    Buy Bananas. Phone the Pope. The handwriting was mine.

Lael's Dream

I flew above the golf course. I did it sitting up.
    Then, lying on my side I scooted high above the lake.
It was easy, and I wished I'd tried it long, long, long ago,
    despite the risk of losing power, and the crash before I wake.

Merla's Dream

My hair was very curly, and it was made of yarn.
    Roy said it was lovely. And all my friends were green
with envy. It never needed cutting, didn't shrink when washed
    in Woolite. Brushing every night kept it fluffy and clean.

Spencer's Dream

        Daddy held me on his knee
            and showed me I had five
        on each hand: one fumb, four
            thingers. We
        played cake. He told me more,
            said I had toes
        on my hind feet.
            I sucked one of those.
        It was the BIG-
            gest, named This Little Pig.

Dori's Dream

Some sort of museum. Bright paintings on the walls.
    No. Wait. They were crazy quilts. In Idaho, I think.
We had come to an auction. Dan liked a tasseled one
    with a wide brown border, but I chose the white and pink.

Ricky's Dream

The orchestra began to play, the curtains parted. I
    entered dressed in purple tights. I leaped to center stage.
One by one I had to lift twelve ballerinas on their toes,
    each spitting asterisks to mark the footnotes on a page.

Lisa's Dream

I started to make a fancy birthday cake. Somehow
    I can't remember who it was for. The doorbell rang.
Just then, a nightingale swooped through the open skylight
    and perched on the chandelier. He sang and sang and sang.

Jay's Dream

Two of our goats broke tether and got into the lucerne.
    It was the Fourth of July. We were all away in town.
I saw a bloated white balloon swaying low in the moonlight.
    Another had just exploded, shreds of it falling down.

Caitlin's Dream

There was a contest. The questions were: 1. What's smoother?
    A rose petal ( ) A kitten's nose ( ) A spoonful of whipped cream ( )
2. What would you rather do? Go swimming ( ) Shopping ( ) Watch TV ( )
    3. If you knew it would come true tomorrow, what would be your
      dream?

Julia's Dream

I was trying to learn the computer. A square knob lit up
    marked GO. So I pressed it. A clanging heap of money

landed in my lap, over ninety dollars worth of heavy coin.
    Someone gave me a plastic bucket. I laughed 'til my nose was runny.

Kippy's Dream

I lay on a velvet bed, and the bed stood out in a field.
    The sun was warm, the wind blew gently, lifting my filmy dress.
Then I was a mermaid on the sea, flipping a sequined tail.
    I need never again live in a house. This was happiness.

Daniel and Michael's Dream

We sometimes dream the same dream, and at the same speed.
    And we can switch identities in sleep, being twins.
Mike can be Dan, and Dan be Mike, at least for part of the night,
    grabbing each other's virtues, shrugging off our sins.
As Daniel, I dreamed an angel held me by the ear, as Michael
    climbed into the lion's den. As Michael I had a dream
that I inhaled Daniel up out of the lion's jaws with my golden
    trumpet, and set him on a cloud. Yes, we're quite a team!

May's Second Dream

Virginia's diary of the future, Lael's flight, Merla's hair
    of sunny yarn, Baby Spencer's hands and feet, Doris's quilt
of colored scraps, Rick the ballet dancer, Lisa's nightingale,
    Jay's two goats, Caitlin's contest, Julia's jackpot and
Kippy the mermaid. As for the Twins: an angel, an ear, a lion's
    jaw, a trumpet and a cloud. Twelve dreams I juggled
through the night, like walking a highwire without a net.
    Well, really, thirteen, I say aloud. Glad it's morning at last,
and a bright one. To myself, and to all the family, I say:
    Here's love! Have a good day!

My Name Was Called

I didn't know what would be done with me.
When my name was called. As when baptized
for the first time. A stiff black four-
cornered hat on. Afraid it would fall off.
My ears stuck out but couldn't grab to keep
it steady on my head slippery and small.
Wet and white the slick enamelled chair,
its pattern of holes in the metal seat
where the water drained. My spotted hand
went up to try to help to bring the velvet
investiture over my square-hatted head.
Awkward. Old bobble with straight short
hair, lashless eyes and smileless mouth.
My name was called. Heavy medallion on wide
blue ribbon hung swinging from my neck.
The Elder's white robe sloshed at his knees,
he held my wrists to my chest, backwards
pressed me under, dipped me blind in the
marble font under green-veined water.
My name was called. My eight-year-old head
didn't know what would be done.

Old teetering monkeylike babylike head
under black gold-tasselled stiff platter-
like hat, sixty years later, the naked ears
stick out. My name is called. Pulled up,
out of the deafening bubbles, boosted up
to sit in the white chair. Murmured over

my head the rapid redundant prayer. Wet
head bowed beneath the hands laid heavy there.
Warm, suggestively wet, my white ruffled
panties streamed in the slick seat.
The silk and velvet lifted. My spotted
hand went up. Awkward. Huge in merciless
light my face on TV in front of my
actual face. My little ignorant ugly patient
helpless head on screen the freshest horror.
The greatest honor. Forced to confront,
but not forced to smile. Child eyes behind
old pouched lashless eyes, never again able
to soften the truth of my future face.
Face immersed, but still afloat over the years.
Head pressed under and blessed. Pulled up
and invested. I didn't know what would be
done, in the white dress or in the black,
when my name was called.

A Day Is Laid By

A day is laid by
It came to pass
Wind is drained
from the willow

Dusk interlaces
the grass
Out of the husk
of twilight
emerges the moon

This the aftermath
of jaded sunset
of noon
and the sirens of bees

Day and wrath
are faded
Now above the bars
of lonely pastures
loom the sacred stars

Flying Home From Utah

Forests are branches of a tree lying down,
its blurred trunk in the north.
Farms are fitted pieces of a floor,

tan and green tiles that get smoother,
smaller, the higher we fly.
Heel-shaped dents of water I know are deep

from here appear opaque, of bluish glass.
Curl after curl, rivers are course locks
unraveling southward over the land;

hills, rubbed felt, crumpled bumps
of antlers pricking from young bucks' heads.
Now towns are scratches here and there

on a wide, brown-bristled hide.
Long roads rayed out from the sores of cities
begin to fester and crawl with light—

above them the plane is a passing insect
that eyes down there remark, forget
in the moment it specks the overcast.

It climbs higher. Clouds become ground.
Pillows of snow meet, weld into ice.
Alone on a moonlit stainless rink

glides the ghost of a larva, the shadow
of our plane. Lights go on
in the worm-belly where we sit;

it becomes the world, and seems to cease
to travel—only vibrates, stretched out tense
in the tank of night.

The room of my mind replaces the long, lit room.
I dream I point my eye over a leaf
and fascinate my gaze upon its veins:

a sprawled leaf, many-fingered, its radial
ridges limber, green—but curled,
tattered, pocked, the brown palm

nibbled by insects, nestled in by worms:
one leaf of a tree that's one tree of a forest,
that's the branch of the vein of a leaf

of a tree. Perpetual worlds
within, upon, above the world, the world
a leaf within a wilderness of worlds.

The Exchange*

Now my body flat,
the ground breathes.
I'll be the grass.

Populous and mixed is mind.
Earth, take thought.
My mouth, be moss.

Field, go walking.
I, a disk,
will look down with seeming eye.

I will be time
and study to be evening.
You world, be clock.

I will stand,
a tree here,
never to know another spot.

Wind, be motion.
Birds, be passion.
Water, invite me to your bed.

*This poem, in an earlier stanza arrangement, is engraved in the granite bench over May Swenson's grave, Logan, Utah.

Index of Dates

May Swenson kept a master index in which she noted publication information, as well as the date and place she began each of her poems. Those dates and places follow the poems listed here.

Above Bear Lake (August 1973, Sunrise Camp, Logan Canyon, Utah)
Beast (1933, Logan, Utah)
Bison Crossing Near Mt. Rushmore (Summer 1973, North Dakota)
Bronco Busting, Event #1 (Winter 1973-74, Tucson, Arizona)
Camping in Madera Canyon (March 1974, Tucson, Arizona)
The Centaur (December 1954, New York, New York)
Cumuli (July 1952, Peterboro, New Hampshire)
A Day Is Laid By (1935, Logan, Utah)
Digging in the Garden of Age I Uncover a Live Root (September 12, 1977, Sea Cliff, New York)
Earth Your Dancing Place (1936, Salt Lake City, Utah)
The Exchange (August 6, 1961, Saratoga, New York)
Feel Me (March 4, 1964, New York, New York)
Flying Home from Utah (September 1962, on the plane to New York)
Goodnight (1934, Logan, Utah)
Haymaking (July 1936, in Canada en route from Utah to New York)
I Look at My Hand (March 12, 1961, New York, New York)
Memory of the Future? Prophecy of the Past? (December 11, 1988, Ocean View, Delaware)
Morning at Point Dume (January 22, 1978, Los Angeles, California)
My Face the Night (December 31, 1966, on a plane from Utah to Indiana)
My Name Was Called (June 1987, Logan, Utah)
A Navajo Blanket (Winter 1974-75, Tucson, Arizona)

Night Visits with the Family (1973, Sea Cliff, New York)
Night Visits with the Family II (Spring 1989, Sea Cliff, New York)
Nightly Vision (1939, New York, New York)
The North Rim (Summer 1971, traveling through Zion National Park
    and Grand Canyon National Park)
Overview (June 20, 1969, on a plane to Logan, Utah)
The Poplar's Shadow (November 1954, New York, New York)
Saguaros above Tucson (1978, Los Angeles, California)
The Seed of My Father (May 12, 1963, New York, New York)
Something Goes By (March 1956, New York, New York)
Speed (July 26, 1970, Alberta, Canada)
Summerfall (July 1983, Sea Cliff, New York)
That the Soul May Wax Plump (1974, Tucson, Arizona)
White Mood (1936, Salt Lake City, Utah)

About the Poet

May Swenson was born on May 28, 1913, in Logan, Utah, and died on December 4, 1989, in Ocean View, Delaware. In that lifetime, she worked as a newspaper reporter, ghostwriter, editor, secretary, manuscript reader for New Directions, and poet-in-residence—but always and mainly as a poet. Eleven volumes of her poetry were published during her lifetime. These earned for her much praise from fellow poets, a place in the hearts and minds of poetry lovers, and many awards.

Among the awards she received were the Brandeis University Creative Arts Award, Rockefeller, Guggenheim, and Ford fellowships, the Bollingen Prize for Poetry, a grant from the National Endowment for the Arts, an honorary doctor of letters degree from Utah State University, and a MacArthur Fellowship. She was a member of the American Academy and Institute of Arts and Letters and a chancellor of the Academy of American Poets.

May Swenson is buried in Logan. Her poem, "The Exchange," is engraved in the granite bench over her grave.